# SNOOKER M

# RECORD B(

THIS
BELONGS TO:

_____

_____

STEPHEN COOK
LINBURY PRODUCTIONS
2021

DATE:                VENUE:

FRIENDLY/COMPETITIVE

COMPETITION:

OPPONENT:

NUMBER OF FRAMES:        W/L      SCORE:

HIGH BREAK:           CAREER HIGHEST:

NOTES:

---

DATE:                VENUE:

FRIENDLY/COMPETITIVE

COMPETITION:

OPPONENT:

NUMBER OF FRAMES:        W/L      SCORE:

HIGH BREAK::          CAREER HIGHEST:

NOTES:

DATE:                VENUE:

FRIENDLY/COMPETITIVE

COMPETITION:

OPPONENT:

NUMBER OF FRAMES:          W/L      SCORE:

HIGH BREAK:              CAREER HIGHEST:

NOTES:




DATE:                VENUE:

FRIENDLY/COMPETITIVE

COMPETITION:

OPPONENT:

NUMBER OF FRAMES:          W/L      SCORE:

HIGH BREAK::              CAREER HIGHEST:

NOTES:

DATE:                 VENUE:

FRIENDLY/COMPETITIVE

COMPETITION:

OPPONENT:

NUMBER OF FRAMES:          W/L      SCORE:

HIGH BREAK:            CAREER HIGHEST:

NOTES:

---

DATE:                 VENUE:

FRIENDLY/COMPETITIVE

COMPETITION:

OPPONENT:

NUMBER OF FRAMES:          W/L      SCORE:

HIGH BREAK::           CAREER HIGHEST:

NOTES:

DATE:                VENUE:

FRIENDLY/COMPETITIVE

COMPETITION:

OPPONENT:

NUMBER OF FRAMES:        W/L      SCORE:

HIGH BREAK:          CAREER HIGHEST:

NOTES:

DATE:                VENUE:

FRIENDLY/COMPETITIVE

COMPETITION:

OPPONENT:

NUMBER OF FRAMES:        W/L      SCORE:

HIGH BREAK::          CAREER HIGHEST:

NOTES:

DATE:                VENUE:

FRIENDLY/COMPETITIVE

COMPETITION:

OPPONENT:

NUMBER OF FRAMES:            W/L       SCORE:

HIGH BREAK:            CAREER HIGHEST:

NOTES:

---

DATE:                VENUE:

FRIENDLY/COMPETITIVE

COMPETITION:

OPPONENT:

NUMBER OF FRAMES:            W/L       SCORE:

HIGH BREAK::            CAREER HIGHEST:

NOTES:

DATE:        VENUE:

FRIENDLY/COMPETITIVE

COMPETITION:

OPPONENT:

NUMBER OF FRAMES:      W/L     SCORE:

HIGH BREAK:        CAREER HIGHEST:

NOTES:

DATE:        VENUE:

FRIENDLY/COMPETITIVE

COMPETITION:

OPPONENT:

NUMBER OF FRAMES:      W/L     SCORE:

HIGH BREAK::        CAREER HIGHEST:

NOTES:

DATE:    VENUE:

FRIENDLY/COMPETITIVE

COMPETITION:

OPPONENT:

NUMBER OF FRAMES:  W/L  SCORE:

HIGH BREAK:   CAREER HIGHEST:

NOTES:



DATE:    VENUE:

FRIENDLY/COMPETITIVE

COMPETITION:

OPPONENT:

NUMBER OF FRAMES:  W/L  SCORE:

HIGH BREAK::   CAREER HIGHEST:

NOTES:

DATE:                VENUE:

FRIENDLY/COMPETITIVE

COMPETITION:

OPPONENT:

NUMBER OF FRAMES:          W/L      SCORE:

HIGH BREAK:              CAREER HIGHEST:

NOTES:

DATE:                VENUE:

FRIENDLY/COMPETITIVE

COMPETITION:

OPPONENT:

NUMBER OF FRAMES:          W/L      SCORE:

HIGH BREAK::             CAREER HIGHEST:

NOTES:

DATE:                    VENUE:

### FRIENDLY/COMPETITIVE

COMPETITION:

OPPONENT:

NUMBER OF FRAMES:          W/L      SCORE:

HIGH BREAK:              CAREER HIGHEST:

NOTES:

---

DATE:                    VENUE:

### FRIENDLY/COMPETITIVE

COMPETITION:

OPPONENT:

NUMBER OF FRAMES:          W/L      SCORE:

HIGH BREAK::              CAREER HIGHEST:

NOTES:

DATE:                    VENUE:

FRIENDLY/COMPETITIVE

COMPETITION:

OPPONENT:

NUMBER OF FRAMES:          W/L        SCORE:

HIGH BREAK:                CAREER HIGHEST:

NOTES:



---

DATE:                    VENUE:

FRIENDLY/COMPETITIVE

COMPETITION:

OPPONENT:

NUMBER OF FRAMES:          W/L        SCORE:

HIGH BREAK::               CAREER HIGHEST:

NOTES:

DATE:                    VENUE:

FRIENDLY/COMPETITIVE

COMPETITION:

OPPONENT:

NUMBER OF FRAMES:           W/L        SCORE:

HIGH BREAK:                CAREER HIGHEST:

NOTES:




---

DATE:                    VENUE:

FRIENDLY/COMPETITIVE

COMPETITION:

OPPONENT:

NUMBER OF FRAMES:           W/L        SCORE:

HIGH BREAK::               CAREER HIGHEST:

NOTES:

DATE:                VENUE:

FRIENDLY/COMPETITIVE

COMPETITION:

OPPONENT:

NUMBER OF FRAMES:        W/L      SCORE:

HIGH BREAK:           CAREER HIGHEST:

NOTES:

DATE:                VENUE:

FRIENDLY/COMPETITIVE

COMPETITION:

OPPONENT:

NUMBER OF FRAMES:        W/L      SCORE:

HIGH BREAK::          CAREER HIGHEST:

NOTES:

DATE:          VENUE:

## FRIENDLY/COMPETITIVE

COMPETITION:

OPPONENT:

NUMBER OF FRAMES:      W/L     SCORE:

HIGH BREAK:       CAREER HIGHEST:

NOTES:

---

DATE:          VENUE:

## FRIENDLY/COMPETITIVE

COMPETITION:

OPPONENT:

NUMBER OF FRAMES:      W/L     SCORE:

HIGH BREAK::       CAREER HIGHEST:

NOTES:

DATE:                    VENUE:

FRIENDLY/COMPETITIVE

COMPETITION:

OPPONENT:

NUMBER OF FRAMES:          W/L      SCORE:

HIGH BREAK:            CAREER HIGHEST:

NOTES:

DATE:                    VENUE:

FRIENDLY/COMPETITIVE

COMPETITION:

OPPONENT:

NUMBER OF FRAMES:          W/L      SCORE:

HIGH BREAK::            CAREER HIGHEST:

NOTES:

DATE:                VENUE:

FRIENDLY/COMPETITIVE

COMPETITION:

OPPONENT:

NUMBER OF FRAMES:          W/L     SCORE:

HIGH BREAK:           CAREER HIGHEST:

NOTES:




DATE:                VENUE:

FRIENDLY/COMPETITIVE

COMPETITION:

OPPONENT:

NUMBER OF FRAMES:          W/L     SCORE:

HIGH BREAK::          CAREER HIGHEST:

NOTES:

DATE:                    VENUE:

FRIENDLY/COMPETITIVE

COMPETITION:

OPPONENT:

NUMBER OF FRAMES:          W/L        SCORE:

HIGH BREAK:              CAREER HIGHEST:

NOTES:

_____

_____

DATE:                    VENUE:

FRIENDLY/COMPETITIVE

COMPETITION:

OPPONENT:

NUMBER OF FRAMES:          W/L        SCORE:

HIGH BREAK::              CAREER HIGHEST:

NOTES:

_____

_____

DATE:                VENUE:

### FRIENDLY/COMPETITIVE

COMPETITION:

OPPONENT:

NUMBER OF FRAMES:        W/L      SCORE:

HIGH BREAK:            CAREER HIGHEST:

NOTES:

DATE:                VENUE:

### FRIENDLY/COMPETITIVE

COMPETITION:

OPPONENT:

NUMBER OF FRAMES:        W/L      SCORE:

HIGH BREAK::           CAREER HIGHEST:

NOTES:

DATE:                VENUE:

FRIENDLY/COMPETITIVE

COMPETITION:

OPPONENT:

NUMBER OF FRAMES:        W/L      SCORE:

HIGH BREAK:              CAREER HIGHEST:

NOTES:

DATE:                VENUE:

FRIENDLY/COMPETITIVE

COMPETITION:

OPPONENT:

NUMBER OF FRAMES:        W/L      SCORE:

HIGH BREAK::             CAREER HIGHEST:

NOTES:

DATE:                    VENUE:

                    FRIENDLY/COMPETITIVE

COMPETITION:

OPPONENT:

NUMBER OF FRAMES:          W/L      SCORE:

HIGH BREAK:              CAREER HIGHEST:

NOTES:




---

DATE:                    VENUE:

                    FRIENDLY/COMPETITIVE

COMPETITION:

OPPONENT:

NUMBER OF FRAMES:          W/L      SCORE:

HIGH BREAK::             CAREER HIGHEST:

NOTES:

DATE:                VENUE:

FRIENDLY/COMPETITIVE

COMPETITION:

OPPONENT:

NUMBER OF FRAMES:          W/L      SCORE:

HIGH BREAK:            CAREER HIGHEST:

NOTES:

DATE:                VENUE:

FRIENDLY/COMPETITIVE

COMPETITION:

OPPONENT:

NUMBER OF FRAMES:          W/L      SCORE:

HIGH BREAK::            CAREER HIGHEST:

NOTES:

DATE:         VENUE:

FRIENDLY/COMPETITIVE

COMPETITION:

OPPONENT:

NUMBER OF FRAMES:      W/L    SCORE:

HIGH BREAK:        CAREER HIGHEST:

NOTES:

---

DATE:         VENUE:

FRIENDLY/COMPETITIVE

COMPETITION:

OPPONENT:

NUMBER OF FRAMES:      W/L    SCORE:

HIGH BREAK::        CAREER HIGHEST:

NOTES:

DATE:                VENUE:

FRIENDLY/COMPETITIVE

COMPETITION:

OPPONENT:

NUMBER OF FRAMES:        W/L        SCORE:

HIGH BREAK:            CAREER HIGHEST:

NOTES:

---

DATE:                VENUE:

FRIENDLY/COMPETITIVE

COMPETITION:

OPPONENT:

NUMBER OF FRAMES:        W/L        SCORE:

HIGH BREAK::            CAREER HIGHEST:

NOTES:

DATE:                VENUE:

FRIENDLY/COMPETITIVE

COMPETITION:

OPPONENT:

NUMBER OF FRAMES:        W/L      SCORE:

HIGH BREAK:              CAREER HIGHEST:

NOTES:

---

DATE:                VENUE:

FRIENDLY/COMPETITIVE

COMPETITION:

OPPONENT:

NUMBER OF FRAMES:        W/L      SCORE:

HIGH BREAK:              CAREER HIGHEST:

NOTES:

DATE:                    VENUE:

FRIENDLY/COMPETITIVE

COMPETITION:

OPPONENT:

NUMBER OF FRAMES:          W/L      SCORE:

HIGH BREAK:             CAREER HIGHEST:

NOTES:

DATE:                    VENUE:

FRIENDLY/COMPETITIVE

COMPETITION:

OPPONENT:

NUMBER OF FRAMES:          W/L      SCORE:

HIGH BREAK::            CAREER HIGHEST:

NOTES:

DATE:                    VENUE:

FRIENDLY/COMPETITIVE

COMPETITION:

OPPONENT:

NUMBER OF FRAMES:           W/L      SCORE:

HIGH BREAK:           CAREER HIGHEST:

NOTES:

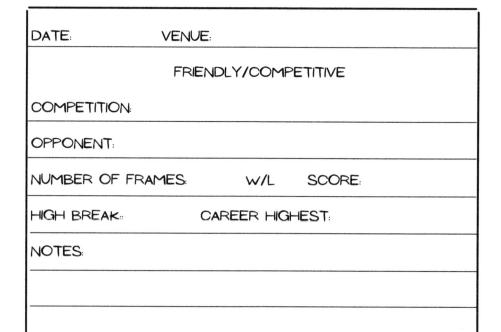

DATE:                    VENUE:

FRIENDLY/COMPETITIVE

COMPETITION:

OPPONENT:

NUMBER OF FRAMES:           W/L      SCORE:

HIGH BREAK:           CAREER HIGHEST:

NOTES:

DATE: VENUE:

FRIENDLY/COMPETITIVE

COMPETITION:

OPPONENT:

NUMBER OF FRAMES: W/L SCORE:

HIGH BREAK: CAREER HIGHEST:

NOTES:

---

DATE: VENUE:

FRIENDLY/COMPETITIVE

COMPETITION:

OPPONENT:

NUMBER OF FRAMES: W/L SCORE:

HIGH BREAK:: CAREER HIGHEST:

NOTES:

DATE:                VENUE:

FRIENDLY/COMPETITIVE

COMPETITION:

OPPONENT:

NUMBER OF FRAMES:          W/L      SCORE:

HIGH BREAK:          CAREER HIGHEST:

NOTES:

---

DATE:                VENUE:

FRIENDLY/COMPETITIVE

COMPETITION:

OPPONENT:

NUMBER OF FRAMES:          W/L      SCORE:

HIGH BREAK:          CAREER HIGHEST.

NOTES:

DATE:                VENUE:

FRIENDLY/COMPETITIVE

COMPETITION:

OPPONENT:

NUMBER OF FRAMES:          W/L        SCORE:

HIGH BREAK:               CAREER HIGHEST:

NOTES:

DATE:                VENUE:

FRIENDLY/COMPETITIVE

COMPETITION:

OPPONENT:

NUMBER OF FRAMES:          W/L        SCORE:

HIGH BREAK::               CAREER HIGHEST:

NOTES:

DATE:                    VENUE:

### FRIENDLY/COMPETITIVE

COMPETITION:

OPPONENT:

NUMBER OF FRAMES:           W/L        SCORE:

HIGH BREAK:              CAREER HIGHEST:

NOTES:

---

DATE:                    VENUE:

### FRIENDLY/COMPETITIVE

COMPETITION:

OPPONENT:

NUMBER OF FRAMES:           W/L        SCORE:

HIGH BREAK::             CAREER HIGHEST:

NOTES:

DATE:        VENUE:

FRIENDLY/COMPETITIVE

COMPETITION:

OPPONENT:

NUMBER OF FRAMES:      W/L     SCORE:

HIGH BREAK:       CAREER HIGHEST:

NOTES:

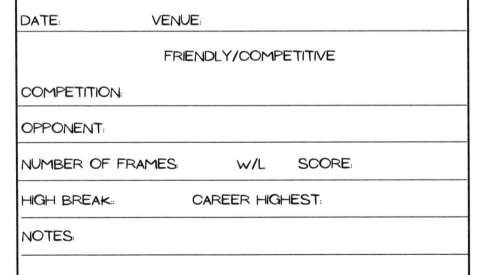

DATE:        VENUE:

FRIENDLY/COMPETITIVE

COMPETITION:

OPPONENT:

NUMBER OF FRAMES:      W/L     SCORE:

HIGH BREAK::       CAREER HIGHEST:

NOTES:

DATE:        VENUE:

FRIENDLY/COMPETITIVE

COMPETITION:

OPPONENT:

NUMBER OF FRAMES:      W/L      SCORE:

HIGH BREAK:      CAREER HIGHEST:

NOTES:

DATE:        VENUE:

FRIENDLY/COMPETITIVE

COMPETITION:

OPPONENT:

NUMBER OF FRAMES:      W/L      SCORE:

HIGH BREAK::      CAREER HIGHEST:

NOTES:

DATE:          VENUE:

FRIENDLY/COMPETITIVE

COMPETITION:

OPPONENT:

NUMBER OF FRAMES:      W/L    SCORE:

HIGH BREAK:      CAREER HIGHEST:

NOTES:

DATE:          VENUE:

FRIENDLY/COMPETITIVE

COMPETITION:

OPPONENT:

NUMBER OF FRAMES:      W/L    SCORE:

HIGH BREAK::      CAREER HIGHEST:

NOTES:

DATE:                    VENUE:

FRIENDLY/COMPETITIVE

COMPETITION:

OPPONENT:

NUMBER OF FRAMES:          W/L     SCORE:

HIGH BREAK:           CAREER HIGHEST:

NOTES:

DATE:                    VENUE:

FRIENDLY/COMPETITIVE

COMPETITION:

OPPONENT:

NUMBER OF FRAMES:          W/L     SCORE:

HIGH BREAK::          CAREER HIGHEST:

NOTES:

DATE:                    VENUE:

FRIENDLY/COMPETITIVE

COMPETITION:

OPPONENT:

NUMBER OF FRAMES:          W/L     SCORE:

HIGH BREAK:          CAREER HIGHEST:

NOTES:


---

DATE:                    VENUE:

FRIENDLY/COMPETITIVE

COMPETITION:

OPPONENT:

NUMBER OF FRAMES:          W/L     SCORE:

HIGH BREAK::          CAREER HIGHEST:

NOTES:

DATE:                    VENUE:

FRIENDLY/COMPETITIVE

COMPETITION:

OPPONENT:

NUMBER OF FRAMES:          W/L      SCORE:

HIGH BREAK:            CAREER HIGHEST:

NOTES:

---

DATE:                    VENUE:

FRIENDLY/COMPETITIVE

COMPETITION:

OPPONENT:

NUMBER OF FRAMES:          W/L      SCORE:

HIGH BREAK::            CAREER HIGHEST:

NOTES:

DATE:                VENUE:
_____

FRIENDLY/COMPETITIVE

COMPETITION:
_____

OPPONENT:
_____

NUMBER OF FRAMES:          W/L      SCORE:
_____

HIGH BREAK:           CAREER HIGHEST:
_____

NOTES:
_____

_____

_____

DATE:                VENUE:
_____

FRIENDLY/COMPETITIVE

COMPETITION:
_____

OPPONENT:
_____

NUMBER OF FRAMES:          W/L      SCORE:
_____

HIGH BREAK::           CAREER HIGHEST:
_____

NOTES:
_____

_____

_____

DATE:                    VENUE:

FRIENDLY/COMPETITIVE

COMPETITION:

OPPONENT:

NUMBER OF FRAMES:          W/L      SCORE:

HIGH BREAK:              CAREER HIGHEST:

NOTES:

---

DATE:                    VENUE:

FRIENDLY/COMPETITIVE

COMPETITION:

OPPONENT:

NUMBER OF FRAMES:          W/L      SCORE:

HIGH BREAK::              CAREER HIGHEST:

NOTES:

DATE:          VENUE:

FRIENDLY/COMPETITIVE

COMPETITION:

OPPONENT:

NUMBER OF FRAMES:      W/L     SCORE:

HIGH BREAK:       CAREER HIGHEST:

NOTES:

DATE:          VENUE:

FRIENDLY/COMPETITIVE

COMPETITION:

OPPONENT:

NUMBER OF FRAMES:      W/L     SCORE:

HIGH BREAK:       CAREER HIGHEST:

NOTES:

DATE: VENUE:

FRIENDLY/COMPETITIVE

COMPETITION:

OPPONENT:

NUMBER OF FRAMES: W/L SCORE:

HIGH BREAK: CAREER HIGHEST:

NOTES:

---

DATE: VENUE:

FRIENDLY/COMPETITIVE

COMPETITION:

OPPONENT:

NUMBER OF FRAMES: W/L SCORE:

HIGH BREAK: CAREER HIGHEST:

NOTES:

DATE:                VENUE:

FRIENDLY/COMPETITIVE

COMPETITION:

OPPONENT:

NUMBER OF FRAMES:        W/L      SCORE:

HIGH BREAK:            CAREER HIGHEST:

NOTES:

DATE:                VENUE:

FRIENDLY/COMPETITIVE

COMPETITION:

OPPONENT:

NUMBER OF FRAMES:        W/L      SCORE:

HIGH BREAK::            CAREER HIGHEST:

NOTES:

DATE:                 VENUE:

FRIENDLY/COMPETITIVE

COMPETITION:

OPPONENT:

NUMBER OF FRAMES:          W/L      SCORE:

HIGH BREAK:              CAREER HIGHEST:

NOTES:




---

DATE:                 VENUE:

FRIENDLY/COMPETITIVE

COMPETITION:

OPPONENT:

NUMBER OF FRAMES:          W/L      SCORE:

HIGH BREAK::             CAREER HIGHEST:

NOTES:

DATE:                  VENUE:

FRIENDLY/COMPETITIVE

COMPETITION:

OPPONENT:

NUMBER OF FRAMES:          W/L      SCORE:

HIGH BREAK:              CAREER HIGHEST:

NOTES:

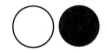

DATE:                  VENUE:

FRIENDLY/COMPETITIVE

COMPETITION:

OPPONENT:

NUMBER OF FRAMES:          W/L      SCORE:

HIGH BREAK::             CAREER HIGHEST:

NOTES:

DATE:                VENUE:

FRIENDLY/COMPETITIVE

COMPETITION:

OPPONENT:

NUMBER OF FRAMES:        W/L      SCORE:

HIGH BREAK:          CAREER HIGHEST:

NOTES:

---

DATE:                VENUE:

FRIENDLY/COMPETITIVE

COMPETITION:

OPPONENT:

NUMBER OF FRAMES:        W/L      SCORE:

HIGH BREAK::         CAREER HIGHEST:

NOTES:

DATE:                VENUE:

FRIENDLY/COMPETITIVE

COMPETITION:

OPPONENT:

NUMBER OF FRAMES:          W/L     SCORE:

HIGH BREAK:              CAREER HIGHEST:

NOTES:

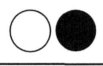

DATE:                VENUE:

FRIENDLY/COMPETITIVE

COMPETITION:

OPPONENT:

NUMBER OF FRAMES:          W/L     SCORE:

HIGH BREAK::              CAREER HIGHEST:

NOTES:

DATE:          VENUE:

FRIENDLY/COMPETITIVE

COMPETITION:

OPPONENT:

NUMBER OF FRAMES:       W/L     SCORE:

HIGH BREAK:         CAREER HIGHEST:

NOTES:

---

DATE:          VENUE:

FRIENDLY/COMPETITIVE

COMPETITION:

OPPONENT:

NUMBER OF FRAMES:       W/L     SCORE:

HIGH BREAK::         CAREER HIGHEST:

NOTES:

DATE:                VENUE:

FRIENDLY/COMPETITIVE

COMPETITION:

OPPONENT:

NUMBER OF FRAMES:        W/L      SCORE:

HIGH BREAK:            CAREER HIGHEST:

NOTES:

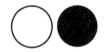

DATE:                VENUE:

FRIENDLY/COMPETITIVE

COMPETITION:

OPPONENT:

NUMBER OF FRAMES:        W/L      SCORE:

HIGH BREAK::          CAREER HIGHEST:

NOTES:

DATE:                    VENUE:

FRIENDLY/COMPETITIVE

COMPETITION:

OPPONENT:

NUMBER OF FRAMES:          W/L     SCORE:

HIGH BREAK:          CAREER HIGHEST:

NOTES:

---

DATE:                    VENUE:

FRIENDLY/COMPETITIVE

COMPETITION:

OPPONENT:

NUMBER OF FRAMES:          W/L     SCORE:

HIGH BREAK::          CAREER HIGHEST:

NOTES:

DATE:                VENUE:

FRIENDLY/COMPETITIVE

COMPETITION:

OPPONENT:

NUMBER OF FRAMES:        W/L     SCORE:

HIGH BREAK:          CAREER HIGHEST:

NOTES:

DATE:                VENUE:

FRIENDLY/COMPETITIVE

COMPETITION:

OPPONENT:

NUMBER OF FRAMES:        W/L     SCORE:

HIGH BREAK::         CAREER HIGHEST:

NOTES:

DATE:                    VENUE:

FRIENDLY/COMPETITIVE

COMPETITION:

OPPONENT:

NUMBER OF FRAMES:          W/L      SCORE:

HIGH BREAK:            CAREER HIGHEST:

NOTES:

---

DATE:                    VENUE:

FRIENDLY/COMPETITIVE

COMPETITION:

OPPONENT:

NUMBER OF FRAMES:          W/L      SCORE:

HIGH BREAK::           CAREER HIGHEST:

NOTES:

DATE:          VENUE:

FRIENDLY/COMPETITIVE

COMPETITION:

OPPONENT:

NUMBER OF FRAMES:     W/L    SCORE:

HIGH BREAK:       CAREER HIGHEST:

NOTES:

DATE:          VENUE:

FRIENDLY/COMPETITIVE

COMPETITION:

OPPONENT:

NUMBER OF FRAMES:     W/L    SCORE:

HIGH BREAK::       CAREER HIGHEST:

NOTES:

DATE:                VENUE:

### FRIENDLY/COMPETITIVE

COMPETITION:

OPPONENT:

NUMBER OF FRAMES:          W/L     SCORE:

HIGH BREAK:          CAREER HIGHEST:

NOTES:

---

DATE:                VENUE:

### FRIENDLY/COMPETITIVE

COMPETITION:

OPPONENT:

NUMBER OF FRAMES:          W/L     SCORE:

HIGH BREAK::          CAREER HIGHEST:

NOTES:

DATE:                VENUE:

FRIENDLY/COMPETITIVE

COMPETITION:

OPPONENT:

NUMBER OF FRAMES:        W/L      SCORE:

HIGH BREAK:             CAREER HIGHEST:

NOTES:

DATE:                VENUE:

FRIENDLY/COMPETITIVE

COMPETITION:

OPPONENT:

NUMBER OF FRAMES:        W/L      SCORE:

HIGH BREAK::            CAREER HIGHEST:

NOTES:

DATE:                VENUE:

FRIENDLY/COMPETITIVE

COMPETITION:

OPPONENT:

NUMBER OF FRAMES:        W/L     SCORE:

HIGH BREAK:           CAREER HIGHEST:

NOTES:

---

DATE:                VENUE:

FRIENDLY/COMPETITIVE

COMPETITION:

OPPONENT:

NUMBER OF FRAMES:        W/L     SCORE:

HIGH BREAK::          CAREER HIGHEST:

NOTES:

DATE:                    VENUE:

FRIENDLY/COMPETITIVE

COMPETITION:

OPPONENT:

NUMBER OF FRAMES:           W/L      SCORE:

HIGH BREAK:              CAREER HIGHEST:

NOTES:




---

DATE:                    VENUE:

FRIENDLY/COMPETITIVE

COMPETITION:

OPPONENT:

NUMBER OF FRAMES:           W/L      SCORE:

HIGH BREAK::             CAREER HIGHEST:

NOTES:

DATE:                    VENUE:

FRIENDLY/COMPETITIVE

COMPETITION:

OPPONENT:

NUMBER OF FRAMES:          W/L      SCORE:

HIGH BREAK:          CAREER HIGHEST:

NOTES:




DATE:                    VENUE:

FRIENDLY/COMPETITIVE

COMPETITION:

OPPONENT:

NUMBER OF FRAMES:          W/L      SCORE:

HIGH BREAK::          CAREER HIGHEST:

NOTES:

DATE:                    VENUE:

FRIENDLY/COMPETITIVE

COMPETITION:

OPPONENT:

NUMBER OF FRAMES:          W/L       SCORE:

HIGH BREAK:              CAREER HIGHEST:

NOTES:

---

DATE:                    VENUE:

FRIENDLY/COMPETITIVE

COMPETITION:

OPPONENT:

NUMBER OF FRAMES:          W/L       SCORE:

HIGH BREAK::              CAREER HIGHEST:

NOTES:

DATE:                    VENUE:

FRIENDLY/COMPETITIVE

COMPETITION:

OPPONENT:

NUMBER OF FRAMES:        W/L      SCORE:

HIGH BREAK:        CAREER HIGHEST:

NOTES:

---

DATE:                    VENUE:

FRIENDLY/COMPETITIVE

COMPETITION:

OPPONENT:

NUMBER OF FRAMES:        W/L      SCORE:

HIGH BREAK::        CAREER HIGHEST:

NOTES:

DATE:                    VENUE:

FRIENDLY/COMPETITIVE

COMPETITION:

OPPONENT:

NUMBER OF FRAMES:          W/L      SCORE:

HIGH BREAK:            CAREER HIGHEST:

NOTES:

DATE:                    VENUE:

FRIENDLY/COMPETITIVE

COMPETITION:

OPPONENT:

NUMBER OF FRAMES:          W/L      SCORE:

HIGH BREAK::            CAREER HIGHEST:

NOTES:

DATE:                VENUE:

FRIENDLY/COMPETITIVE

COMPETITION:

OPPONENT:

NUMBER OF FRAMES:        W/L      SCORE:

HIGH BREAK:              CAREER HIGHEST:

NOTES:

---

DATE:                VENUE:

FRIENDLY/COMPETITIVE

COMPETITION:

OPPONENT:

NUMBER OF FRAMES:        W/L      SCORE:

HIGH BREAK:              CAREER HIGHEST:

NOTES:

DATE:                 VENUE:

FRIENDLY/COMPETITIVE

COMPETITION:

OPPONENT:

NUMBER OF FRAMES:          W/L      SCORE:

HIGH BREAK:           CAREER HIGHEST:

NOTES:

DATE:                 VENUE:

FRIENDLY/COMPETITIVE

COMPETITION:

OPPONENT:

NUMBER OF FRAMES:          W/L      SCORE:

HIGH BREAK::          CAREER HIGHEST:

NOTES:

DATE:                    VENUE:

FRIENDLY/COMPETITIVE

COMPETITION:

OPPONENT:

NUMBER OF FRAMES:          W/L      SCORE:

HIGH BREAK:           CAREER HIGHEST:

NOTES:

---

DATE:                    VENUE:

FRIENDLY/COMPETITIVE

COMPETITION:

OPPONENT:

NUMBER OF FRAMES:          W/L      SCORE:

HIGH BREAK::          CAREER HIGHEST:

NOTES:

DATE:                    VENUE:

FRIENDLY/COMPETITIVE

COMPETITION:

OPPONENT:

NUMBER OF FRAMES:          W/L      SCORE:

HIGH BREAK:              CAREER HIGHEST:

NOTES:

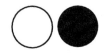

DATE:                    VENUE:

FRIENDLY/COMPETITIVE

COMPETITION:

OPPONENT:

NUMBER OF FRAMES:          W/L      SCORE:

HIGH BREAK::             CAREER HIGHEST:

NOTES:

DATE:                    VENUE:

### FRIENDLY/COMPETITIVE

COMPETITION:

OPPONENT:

NUMBER OF FRAMES:          W/L      SCORE:

HIGH BREAK:            CAREER HIGHEST:

NOTES:

---

DATE:                    VENUE:

### FRIENDLY/COMPETITIVE

COMPETITION:

OPPONENT:

NUMBER OF FRAMES:          W/L      SCORE:

HIGH BREAK::            CAREER HIGHEST:

NOTES:

DATE:                    VENUE:

FRIENDLY/COMPETITIVE

COMPETITION:

OPPONENT:

NUMBER OF FRAMES:           W/L      SCORE:

HIGH BREAK:              CAREER HIGHEST:

NOTES:

DATE:                    VENUE:

FRIENDLY/COMPETITIVE

COMPETITION:

OPPONENT:

NUMBER OF FRAMES:           W/L      SCORE:

HIGH BREAK::              CAREER HIGHEST:

NOTES:

DATE:                VENUE:

FRIENDLY/COMPETITIVE

COMPETITION:

OPPONENT:

NUMBER OF FRAMES:          W/L      SCORE:

HIGH BREAK:           CAREER HIGHEST:

NOTES:

---

DATE:                VENUE:

FRIENDLY/COMPETITIVE

COMPETITION:

OPPONENT:

NUMBER OF FRAMES:          W/L      SCORE:

HIGH BREAK::          CAREER HIGHEST:

NOTES:

DATE:					VENUE:

FRIENDLY/COMPETITIVE

COMPETITION:

OPPONENT:

NUMBER OF FRAMES:			W/L		SCORE:

HIGH BREAK:			CAREER HIGHEST:

NOTES:

DATE:					VENUE:

FRIENDLY/COMPETITIVE

COMPETITION:

OPPONENT:

NUMBER OF FRAMES:			W/L		SCORE:

HIGH BREAK::			CAREER HIGHEST:

NOTES:

DATE:                VENUE:

FRIENDLY/COMPETITIVE

COMPETITION:

OPPONENT:

NUMBER OF FRAMES:          W/L      SCORE:

HIGH BREAK:          CAREER HIGHEST:

NOTES:

---

DATE:                VENUE:

FRIENDLY/COMPETITIVE

COMPETITION:

OPPONENT:

NUMBER OF FRAMES:          W/L      SCORE:

HIGH BREAK:          CAREER HIGHEST:

NOTES:

DATE:                VENUE:

FRIENDLY/COMPETITIVE

COMPETITION:

OPPONENT:

NUMBER OF FRAMES:        W/L      SCORE:

HIGH BREAK:            CAREER HIGHEST:

NOTES:

DATE:                VENUE:

FRIENDLY/COMPETITIVE

COMPETITION:

OPPONENT:

NUMBER OF FRAMES:        W/L      SCORE:

HIGH BREAK::            CAREER HIGHEST:

NOTES:

DATE:                    VENUE:

FRIENDLY/COMPETITIVE

COMPETITION:

OPPONENT:

NUMBER OF FRAMES:          W/L      SCORE:

HIGH BREAK:              CAREER HIGHEST:

NOTES:


---

DATE:                    VENUE:

FRIENDLY/COMPETITIVE

COMPETITION:

OPPONENT:

NUMBER OF FRAMES:          W/L      SCORE:

HIGH BREAK:              CAREER HIGHEST:

NOTES:

DATE:                VENUE:

FRIENDLY/COMPETITIVE

COMPETITION:

OPPONENT:

NUMBER OF FRAMES:        W/L      SCORE:

HIGH BREAK:           CAREER HIGHEST:

NOTES:

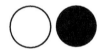

DATE:                VENUE:

FRIENDLY/COMPETITIVE

COMPETITION:

OPPONENT:

NUMBER OF FRAMES:        W/L      SCORE:

HIGH BREAK::          CAREER HIGHEST:

NOTES:

DATE:                VENUE:

FRIENDLY/COMPETITIVE

COMPETITION:

OPPONENT:

NUMBER OF FRAMES:        W/L      SCORE:

HIGH BREAK:            CAREER HIGHEST:

NOTES:

---

DATE:                VENUE:

FRIENDLY/COMPETITIVE

COMPETITION:

OPPONENT:

NUMBER OF FRAMES:        W/L      SCORE:

HIGH BREAK:            CAREER HIGHEST:

NOTES:

DATE:                VENUE:

FRIENDLY/COMPETITIVE

COMPETITION:

OPPONENT:

NUMBER OF FRAMES:        W/L        SCORE:

HIGH BREAK:              CAREER HIGHEST:

NOTES:

DATE:                VENUE:

FRIENDLY/COMPETITIVE

COMPETITION:

OPPONENT:

NUMBER OF FRAMES:        W/L        SCORE:

HIGH BREAK::              CAREER HIGHEST:

NOTES:

DATE:                    VENUE:

FRIENDLY/COMPETITIVE

COMPETITION:

OPPONENT:

NUMBER OF FRAMES:            W/L      SCORE:

HIGH BREAK:              CAREER HIGHEST:

NOTES:

---

DATE:                    VENUE:

FRIENDLY/COMPETITIVE

COMPETITION:

OPPONENT:

NUMBER OF FRAMES:            W/L      SCORE:

HIGH BREAK::              CAREER HIGHEST:

NOTES:

DATE:                    VENUE:

FRIENDLY/COMPETITIVE

COMPETITION:

OPPONENT:

NUMBER OF FRAMES:          W/L      SCORE:

HIGH BREAK:            CAREER HIGHEST:

NOTES:

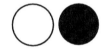

DATE:                    VENUE:

FRIENDLY/COMPETITIVE

COMPETITION:

OPPONENT:

NUMBER OF FRAMES:          W/L      SCORE:

HIGH BREAK::            CAREER HIGHEST:

NOTES:

DATE:                    VENUE:

FRIENDLY/COMPETITIVE

COMPETITION:

OPPONENT:

NUMBER OF FRAMES:          W/L     SCORE:

HIGH BREAK:          CAREER HIGHEST:

NOTES:

---

DATE:                    VENUE:

FRIENDLY/COMPETITIVE

COMPETITION:

OPPONENT:

NUMBER OF FRAMES:          W/L     SCORE:

HIGH BREAK::          CAREER HIGHEST:

NOTES:

DATE:                    VENUE:

FRIENDLY/COMPETITIVE

COMPETITION:

OPPONENT:

NUMBER OF FRAMES:        W/L      SCORE:

HIGH BREAK:              CAREER HIGHEST:

NOTES:

DATE:                    VENUE:

FRIENDLY/COMPETITIVE

COMPETITION:

OPPONENT:

NUMBER OF FRAMES:        W/L      SCORE:

HIGH BREAK::             CAREER HIGHEST:

NOTES:

DATE:                    VENUE:

FRIENDLY/COMPETITIVE

COMPETITION:

OPPONENT:

NUMBER OF FRAMES:          W/L      SCORE:

HIGH BREAK:             CAREER HIGHEST:

NOTES:

---

DATE:                    VENUE:

FRIENDLY/COMPETITIVE

COMPETITION:

OPPONENT:

NUMBER OF FRAMES:          W/L      SCORE:

HIGH BREAK::            CAREER HIGHEST:

NOTES:

DATE:                VENUE:

FRIENDLY/COMPETITIVE

COMPETITION:

OPPONENT:

NUMBER OF FRAMES:          W/L      SCORE:

HIGH BREAK:            CAREER HIGHEST:

NOTES:

---

DATE:                VENUE:

FRIENDLY/COMPETITIVE

COMPETITION:

OPPONENT:

NUMBER OF FRAMES:          W/L      SCORE:

HIGH BREAK::            CAREER HIGHEST:

NOTES:

DATE:        VENUE:

FRIENDLY/COMPETITIVE

COMPETITION:

OPPONENT:

NUMBER OF FRAMES:     W/L    SCORE:

HIGH BREAK:      CAREER HIGHEST:

NOTES:

---

DATE:        VENUE:

FRIENDLY/COMPETITIVE

COMPETITION:

OPPONENT:

NUMBER OF FRAMES:     W/L    SCORE:

HIGH BREAK:      CAREER HIGHEST:

NOTES:

DATE:        VENUE:

FRIENDLY/COMPETITIVE

COMPETITION:

OPPONENT:

NUMBER OF FRAMES:     W/L    SCORE:

HIGH BREAK:     CAREER HIGHEST:

NOTES:

DATE:        VENUE:

FRIENDLY/COMPETITIVE

COMPETITION:

OPPONENT:

NUMBER OF FRAMES:     W/L    SCORE:

HIGH BREAK::     CAREER HIGHEST:

NOTES:

DATE:                VENUE:

FRIENDLY/COMPETITIVE

COMPETITION:

OPPONENT:

NUMBER OF FRAMES:          W/L     SCORE:

HIGH BREAK:            CAREER HIGHEST:

NOTES:

---

DATE:                VENUE:

FRIENDLY/COMPETITIVE

COMPETITION:

OPPONENT:

NUMBER OF FRAMES:          W/L     SCORE:

HIGH BREAK:            CAREER HIGHEST:

NOTES:

DATE:                VENUE:

FRIENDLY/COMPETITIVE

COMPETITION:

OPPONENT:

NUMBER OF FRAMES:          W/L      SCORE:

HIGH BREAK:            CAREER HIGHEST:

NOTES:

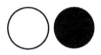

DATE:                VENUE:

FRIENDLY/COMPETITIVE

COMPETITION:

OPPONENT:

NUMBER OF FRAMES:          W/L      SCORE:

HIGH BREAK::           CAREER HIGHEST:

NOTES:

DATE:                VENUE:

FRIENDLY/COMPETITIVE

COMPETITION:

OPPONENT:

NUMBER OF FRAMES:          W/L     SCORE:

HIGH BREAK:              CAREER HIGHEST:

NOTES:

---

DATE:                VENUE:

FRIENDLY/COMPETITIVE

COMPETITION:

OPPONENT:

NUMBER OF FRAMES:          W/L     SCORE:

HIGH BREAK::              CAREER HIGHEST:

NOTES:

DATE:                VENUE:

FRIENDLY/COMPETITIVE

COMPETITION:

OPPONENT:

NUMBER OF FRAMES:        W/L        SCORE:

HIGH BREAK:              CAREER HIGHEST:

NOTES:

---

DATE:                VENUE:

FRIENDLY/COMPETITIVE

COMPETITION:

OPPONENT:

NUMBER OF FRAMES:        W/L        SCORE:

HIGH BREAK::              CAREER HIGHEST:

NOTES:

DATE:                    VENUE:

### FRIENDLY/COMPETITIVE

COMPETITION:

OPPONENT:

NUMBER OF FRAMES:        W/L      SCORE:

HIGH BREAK:              CAREER HIGHEST:

NOTES:


DATE:                    VENUE:

### FRIENDLY/COMPETITIVE

COMPETITION:

OPPONENT:

NUMBER OF FRAMES:        W/L      SCORE:

HIGH BREAK::             CAREER HIGHEST:

NOTES:

DATE:                VENUE:

FRIENDLY/COMPETITIVE

COMPETITION:

OPPONENT:

NUMBER OF FRAMES:         W/L       SCORE:

HIGH BREAK:            CAREER HIGHEST:

NOTES:

DATE:                VENUE:

FRIENDLY/COMPETITIVE

COMPETITION:

OPPONENT:

NUMBER OF FRAMES:         W/L       SCORE:

HIGH BREAK::            CAREER HIGHEST:

NOTES:

DATE:                    VENUE:

FRIENDLY/COMPETITIVE

COMPETITION:

OPPONENT:

NUMBER OF FRAMES:          W/L     SCORE:

HIGH BREAK:          CAREER HIGHEST:

NOTES:

---

DATE:                    VENUE:

FRIENDLY/COMPETITIVE

COMPETITION:

OPPONENT:

NUMBER OF FRAMES:          W/L     SCORE:

HIGH BREAK::          CAREER HIGHEST:

NOTES:

DATE:                VENUE:

FRIENDLY/COMPETITIVE

COMPETITION:

OPPONENT:

NUMBER OF FRAMES:          W/L        SCORE:

HIGH BREAK:              CAREER HIGHEST:

NOTES:

DATE:                VENUE:

FRIENDLY/COMPETITIVE

COMPETITION:

OPPONENT:

NUMBER OF FRAMES:          W/L        SCORE:

HIGH BREAK::             CAREER HIGHEST:

NOTES:

DATE:                VENUE:

FRIENDLY/COMPETITIVE

COMPETITION:

OPPONENT:

NUMBER OF FRAMES:          W/L      SCORE:

HIGH BREAK:              CAREER HIGHEST:

NOTES:

---

DATE:                VENUE:

FRIENDLY/COMPETITIVE

COMPETITION:

OPPONENT:

NUMBER OF FRAMES:          W/L      SCORE:

HIGH BREAK:              CAREER HIGHEST:

NOTES:

DATE:                    VENUE:

FRIENDLY/COMPETITIVE

COMPETITION:

OPPONENT:

NUMBER OF FRAMES:          W/L      SCORE:

HIGH BREAK:              CAREER HIGHEST:

NOTES:

DATE:                    VENUE:

FRIENDLY/COMPETITIVE

COMPETITION:

OPPONENT:

NUMBER OF FRAMES:          W/L      SCORE:

HIGH BREAK::             CAREER HIGHEST:

NOTES:

DATE: VENUE:

FRIENDLY/COMPETITIVE

COMPETITION:

OPPONENT:

NUMBER OF FRAMES: W/L SCORE:

HIGH BREAK: CAREER HIGHEST:

NOTES:

---

DATE: VENUE:

FRIENDLY/COMPETITIVE

COMPETITION:

OPPONENT:

NUMBER OF FRAMES: W/L SCORE:

HIGH BREAK:: CAREER HIGHEST:

NOTES:

DATE:                VENUE:

FRIENDLY/COMPETITIVE

COMPETITION:

OPPONENT:

NUMBER OF FRAMES:        W/L      SCORE:

HIGH BREAK:            CAREER HIGHEST:

NOTES:

---

DATE:                VENUE:

FRIENDLY/COMPETITIVE

COMPETITION:

OPPONENT:

NUMBER OF FRAMES:        W/L      SCORE:

HIGH BREAK::           CAREER HIGHEST:

NOTES:

DATE:                    VENUE:

FRIENDLY/COMPETITIVE

COMPETITION:

OPPONENT:

NUMBER OF FRAMES:          W/L      SCORE:

HIGH BREAK:          CAREER HIGHEST:

NOTES:

---

DATE:                    VENUE:

FRIENDLY/COMPETITIVE

COMPETITION:

OPPONENT:

NUMBER OF FRAMES:          W/L      SCORE:

HIGH BREAK:          CAREER HIGHEST:

NOTES:

DATE:        VENUE:

### FRIENDLY/COMPETITIVE

COMPETITION:

OPPONENT:

NUMBER OF FRAMES:     W/L    SCORE:

HIGH BREAK:     CAREER HIGHEST:

NOTES:

DATE:        VENUE:

### FRIENDLY/COMPETITIVE

COMPETITION:

OPPONENT:

NUMBER OF FRAMES:     W/L    SCORE:

HIGH BREAK::     CAREER HIGHEST:

NOTES:

DATE:                    VENUE:

FRIENDLY/COMPETITIVE

COMPETITION:

OPPONENT:

NUMBER OF FRAMES:         W/L      SCORE:

HIGH BREAK:          CAREER HIGHEST:

NOTES:

---

DATE:                    VENUE:

FRIENDLY/COMPETITIVE

COMPETITION:

OPPONENT:

NUMBER OF FRAMES:         W/L      SCORE:

HIGH BREAK::         CAREER HIGHEST:

NOTES:

DATE:                    VENUE:

FRIENDLY/COMPETITIVE

COMPETITION:

OPPONENT:

NUMBER OF FRAMES:          W/L       SCORE:

HIGH BREAK:          CAREER HIGHEST:

NOTES:

---

DATE:                    VENUE:

FRIENDLY/COMPETITIVE

COMPETITION:

OPPONENT:

NUMBER OF FRAMES:          W/L       SCORE:

HIGH BREAK::          CAREER HIGHEST:

NOTES:

DATE:                    VENUE:

FRIENDLY/COMPETITIVE

COMPETITION:

OPPONENT:

NUMBER OF FRAMES:          W/L      SCORE:

HIGH BREAK:              CAREER HIGHEST:

NOTES:

---

DATE:                    VENUE:

FRIENDLY/COMPETITIVE

COMPETITION:

OPPONENT:

NUMBER OF FRAMES:          W/L      SCORE:

HIGH BREAK::             CAREER HIGHEST:

NOTES:

DATE:                    VENUE:

FRIENDLY/COMPETITIVE

COMPETITION:

OPPONENT:

NUMBER OF FRAMES:          W/L      SCORE:

HIGH BREAK:          CAREER HIGHEST:

NOTES:

DATE:                    VENUE:

FRIENDLY/COMPETITIVE

COMPETITION:

OPPONENT:

NUMBER OF FRAMES:          W/L      SCORE:

HIGH BREAK::          CAREER HIGHEST:

NOTES:

DATE:                VENUE:

FRIENDLY/COMPETITIVE

COMPETITION:

OPPONENT:

NUMBER OF FRAMES:        W/L     SCORE:

HIGH BREAK:           CAREER HIGHEST:

NOTES:




DATE:                VENUE:

FRIENDLY/COMPETITIVE

COMPETITION:

OPPONENT:

NUMBER OF FRAMES:        W/L     SCORE:

HIGH BREAK::          CAREER HIGHEST:

NOTES:

DATE:                VENUE:

FRIENDLY/COMPETITIVE

COMPETITION:

OPPONENT:

NUMBER OF FRAMES:        W/L      SCORE:

HIGH BREAK:          CAREER HIGHEST:

NOTES:




DATE:                VENUE:

FRIENDLY/COMPETITIVE

COMPETITION:

OPPONENT:

NUMBER OF FRAMES:        W/L      SCORE:

HIGH BREAK::          CAREER HIGHEST:

NOTES:

DATE:                    VENUE:

FRIENDLY/COMPETITIVE

COMPETITION:

OPPONENT:

NUMBER OF FRAMES:          W/L      SCORE:

HIGH BREAK:          CAREER HIGHEST:

NOTES:




DATE:                    VENUE:

FRIENDLY/COMPETITIVE

COMPETITION:

OPPONENT:

NUMBER OF FRAMES:          W/L      SCORE:

HIGH BREAK::          CAREER HIGHEST:

NOTES:

DATE:                VENUE:

FRIENDLY/COMPETITIVE

COMPETITION:

OPPONENT:

NUMBER OF FRAMES:        W/L      SCORE:

HIGH BREAK:            CAREER HIGHEST:

NOTES:

DATE:                VENUE:

FRIENDLY/COMPETITIVE

COMPETITION:

OPPONENT:

NUMBER OF FRAMES:        W/L      SCORE:

HIGH BREAK::            CAREER HIGHEST:

NOTES:

DATE:                 VENUE:

FRIENDLY/COMPETITIVE

COMPETITION:

OPPONENT:

NUMBER OF FRAMES:          W/L      SCORE:

HIGH BREAK:               CAREER HIGHEST:

NOTES:

---

DATE:                 VENUE:

FRIENDLY/COMPETITIVE

COMPETITION:

OPPONENT:

NUMBER OF FRAMES:          W/L      SCORE:

HIGH BREAK::              CAREER HIGHEST:

NOTES:

DATE:                VENUE:

FRIENDLY/COMPETITIVE

COMPETITION:

OPPONENT:

NUMBER OF FRAMES:          W/L      SCORE:

HIGH BREAK:              CAREER HIGHEST:

NOTES:

DATE:                VENUE:

FRIENDLY/COMPETITIVE

COMPETITION:

OPPONENT:

NUMBER OF FRAMES:          W/L      SCORE:

HIGH BREAK::              CAREER HIGHEST:

NOTES:

DATE:                VENUE:

FRIENDLY/COMPETITIVE

COMPETITION:

OPPONENT:

NUMBER OF FRAMES:        W/L      SCORE:

HIGH BREAK:           CAREER HIGHEST:

NOTES:

---

DATE:                VENUE:

FRIENDLY/COMPETITIVE

COMPETITION:

OPPONENT:

NUMBER OF FRAMES:        W/L      SCORE:

HIGH BREAK::          CAREER HIGHEST:

NOTES:

DATE:                VENUE:

FRIENDLY/COMPETITIVE

COMPETITION:

OPPONENT:

NUMBER OF FRAMES:          W/L      SCORE:

HIGH BREAK:              CAREER HIGHEST:

NOTES:

DATE:                VENUE:

FRIENDLY/COMPETITIVE

COMPETITION:

OPPONENT:

NUMBER OF FRAMES:          W/L      SCORE:

HIGH BREAK::             CAREER HIGHEST:

NOTES:

DATE:                VENUE:

FRIENDLY/COMPETITIVE

COMPETITION:

OPPONENT:

NUMBER OF FRAMES:          W/L      SCORE:

HIGH BREAK:              CAREER HIGHEST:

NOTES:

---

DATE:                VENUE:

FRIENDLY/COMPETITIVE

COMPETITION:

OPPONENT:

NUMBER OF FRAMES:          W/L      SCORE:

HIGH BREAK::              CAREER HIGHEST:

NOTES:

DATE:                VENUE:

FRIENDLY/COMPETITIVE

COMPETITION:

OPPONENT:

NUMBER OF FRAMES:          W/L      SCORE:

HIGH BREAK:            CAREER HIGHEST:

NOTES:

---

DATE:                VENUE:

FRIENDLY/COMPETITIVE

COMPETITION:

OPPONENT:

NUMBER OF FRAMES:          W/L      SCORE:

HIGH BREAK::            CAREER HIGHEST:

NOTES:

DATE:                VENUE:

FRIENDLY/COMPETITIVE

COMPETITION:

OPPONENT:

NUMBER OF FRAMES:          W/L      SCORE:

HIGH BREAK:          CAREER HIGHEST:

NOTES:

---

DATE:                VENUE:

FRIENDLY/COMPETITIVE

COMPETITION:

OPPONENT:

NUMBER OF FRAMES:          W/L      SCORE:

HIGH BREAK::          CAREER HIGHEST:

NOTES:

DATE:                VENUE:

FRIENDLY/COMPETITIVE

COMPETITION:

OPPONENT:

NUMBER OF FRAMES:        W/L      SCORE:

HIGH BREAK:            CAREER HIGHEST:

NOTES:

DATE:                VENUE:

FRIENDLY/COMPETITIVE

COMPETITION:

OPPONENT:

NUMBER OF FRAMES:        W/L      SCORE:

HIGH BREAK::            CAREER HIGHEST:

NOTES:

DATE:                VENUE:

FRIENDLY/COMPETITIVE

COMPETITION:

OPPONENT:

NUMBER OF FRAMES:          W/L      SCORE:

HIGH BREAK:            CAREER HIGHEST:

NOTES:

---

DATE:                VENUE:

FRIENDLY/COMPETITIVE

COMPETITION:

OPPONENT:

NUMBER OF FRAMES:          W/L      SCORE:

HIGH BREAK:            CAREER HIGHEST:

NOTES:

DATE:                VENUE:

FRIENDLY/COMPETITIVE

COMPETITION:

OPPONENT:

NUMBER OF FRAMES:        W/L      SCORE:

HIGH BREAK:              CAREER HIGHEST:

NOTES:

DATE:                VENUE:

FRIENDLY/COMPETITIVE

COMPETITION:

OPPONENT:

NUMBER OF FRAMES:        W/L      SCORE:

HIGH BREAK::              CAREER HIGHEST:

NOTES:

DATE:                VENUE:

### FRIENDLY/COMPETITIVE

COMPETITION:

OPPONENT:

NUMBER OF FRAMES:        W/L      SCORE:

HIGH BREAK:              CAREER HIGHEST:

NOTES:




---

DATE:                VENUE:

### FRIENDLY/COMPETITIVE

COMPETITION:

OPPONENT:

NUMBER OF FRAMES:        W/L      SCORE:

HIGH BREAK::             CAREER HIGHEST:

NOTES:

DATE:                VENUE:

FRIENDLY/COMPETITIVE

COMPETITION:

OPPONENT:

NUMBER OF FRAMES:          W/L      SCORE:

HIGH BREAK:              CAREER HIGHEST:

NOTES:

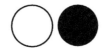

DATE:                VENUE:

FRIENDLY/COMPETITIVE

COMPETITION:

OPPONENT:

NUMBER OF FRAMES:          W/L      SCORE:

HIGH BREAK::              CAREER HIGHEST:

NOTES:

DATE:                VENUE:

FRIENDLY/COMPETITIVE

COMPETITION:

OPPONENT:

NUMBER OF FRAMES:          W/L     SCORE:

HIGH BREAK:          CAREER HIGHEST:

NOTES:


---

DATE:                VENUE:

FRIENDLY/COMPETITIVE

COMPETITION:

OPPONENT:

NUMBER OF FRAMES:          W/L     SCORE:

HIGH BREAK::          CAREER HIGHEST:

NOTES:

DATE:                    VENUE:

FRIENDLY/COMPETITIVE

COMPETITION:

OPPONENT:

NUMBER OF FRAMES:          W/L       SCORE:

HIGH BREAK:            CAREER HIGHEST:

NOTES:

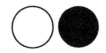

DATE:                    VENUE:

FRIENDLY/COMPETITIVE

COMPETITION:

OPPONENT:

NUMBER OF FRAMES:          W/L       SCORE:

HIGH BREAK::            CAREER HIGHEST:

NOTES:

DATE:                VENUE:

### FRIENDLY/COMPETITIVE

COMPETITION:

OPPONENT:

NUMBER OF FRAMES:        W/L        SCORE:

HIGH BREAK:          CAREER HIGHEST:

NOTES:

---

DATE:                VENUE:

### FRIENDLY/COMPETITIVE

COMPETITION:

OPPONENT:

NUMBER OF FRAMES:        W/L        SCORE:

HIGH BREAK::          CAREER HIGHEST:

NOTES:

DATE:                    VENUE:

FRIENDLY/COMPETITIVE

COMPETITION:

OPPONENT:

NUMBER OF FRAMES:          W/L      SCORE:

HIGH BREAK:              CAREER HIGHEST:

NOTES:

DATE:                    VENUE:

FRIENDLY/COMPETITIVE

COMPETITION:

OPPONENT:

NUMBER OF FRAMES:          W/L      SCORE:

HIGH BREAK::              CAREER HIGHEST:

NOTES:

DATE:                VENUE:

FRIENDLY/COMPETITIVE

COMPETITION:

OPPONENT:

NUMBER OF FRAMES:        W/L      SCORE:

HIGH BREAK:          CAREER HIGHEST:

NOTES:

---

DATE:                VENUE:

FRIENDLY/COMPETITIVE

COMPETITION:

OPPONENT:

NUMBER OF FRAMES:        W/L      SCORE:

HIGH BREAK::          CAREER HIGHEST:

NOTES:

DATE:                    VENUE:

FRIENDLY/COMPETITIVE

COMPETITION:

OPPONENT:

NUMBER OF FRAMES:          W/L      SCORE:

HIGH BREAK:          CAREER HIGHEST:

NOTES:

DATE:                    VENUE:

FRIENDLY/COMPETITIVE

COMPETITION:

OPPONENT:

NUMBER OF FRAMES:          W/L      SCORE:

HIGH BREAK::          CAREER HIGHEST:

NOTES:

Printed in Great Britain
by Amazon

76731196R00072